American Government

Local Governments

by Connor Stratton

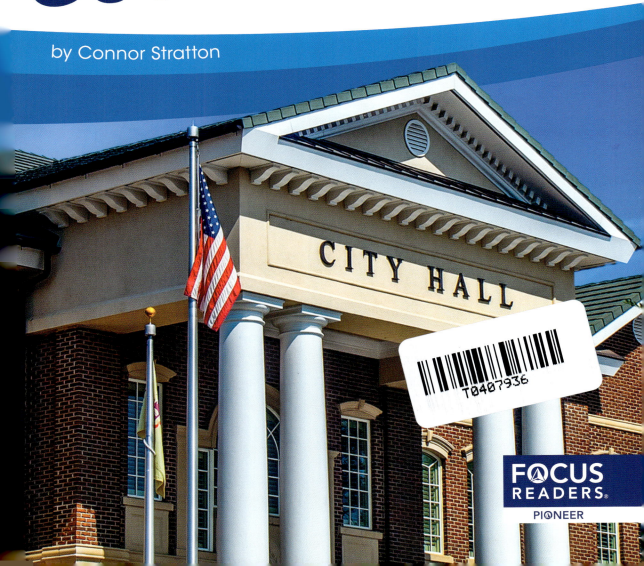

www.focusreaders.com

Copyright © 2024 by Focus Readers®, Lake Elmo, MN 55042. All rights reserved. No part of this book may be reproduced or utilized in any form or by any means without written permission from the publisher.

Focus Readers is distributed by North Star Editions:
sales@northstareditions.com | 888-417-0195

Produced for Focus Readers by Red Line Editorial.

Photographs ©: Shutterstock Images, cover, 1, 4, 7, 11, 12, 15; iStockphoto, 8, 17; M. Spencer Green/AP Images, 18; Red Line Editorial, 21

Library of Congress Cataloging-in-Publication Data
Names: Stratton, Connor, author.
Title: Local governments / by Connor Stratton.
Description: Lake Elmo, MN : Focus Readers, [2024] | Series: American
   government | Includes bibliographical references and index. | Audience:
   Grades 2-3
Identifiers: LCCN 2023002924 (print) | LCCN 2023002925 (ebook) | ISBN
   9781637395912 (hardcover) | ISBN 9781637396483 (paperback) | ISBN
   9781637397619 (ebook pdf) | ISBN 9781637397053 (hosted ebook)
Subjects: LCSH: Local government--United States--Juvenile literature. |
   Municipal government--United States--Juvenile literature.
Classification: LCC JS331 .S78 2024 (print) | LCC JS331 (ebook) | DDC
   320.80973--dc23/eng/20230213
LC record available at https://lccn.loc.gov/2023002924
LC ebook record available at https://lccn.loc.gov/2023002925

Printed in the United States of America
Mankato, MN
082023

About the Author

Connor Stratton writes and edits nonfiction children's books. He lives in Minnesota.

Table of Contents

CHAPTER 1

Governments Close By 5

CHAPTER 2

Counties 9

CHAPTER 3

Cities and Towns 13

A CLOSER LOOK

Why Local Government Matters 16

CHAPTER 4

One Job 19

Focus on Local Governments • 22
Glossary • 23
To Learn More • 24
Index • 24

Chapter 1

Governments Close By

The United States has a **government**. States have governments, too. So do smaller places. **Local** governments take care of people close by.

Local governments do many things. They make **laws**. They run parks. They help local businesses. Many local governments run buses and trains. Many deal with trash. They often take care of water, too.

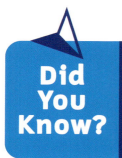

Did You Know? Young adults can lead local governments. Some leaders are just 18 years old.

Chapter 2

Counties

County governments are one kind of local government. A **board** often leads a county. People in the county pick board members. They vote in an **election**.

Counties have many jobs. They set **taxes**. They care for roads. Counties keep records, too. They keep track of buildings. They track people's health. Counties also have courts. Many have libraries. Some have hospitals.

Did You Know? Louisiana has parishes instead of counties. Alaska has boroughs.

Chapter 3

Cities and Towns

A county can have many towns and cities. Each town or city has a government. The leader is often called a mayor. People elect their mayor.

Councils often work with mayors. They make new laws. Council members also **represent** parts of their city. People may face problems. They can tell their council member. That person can help fix the problem.

Did You Know? Some cities have millions of people. Towns can be home to just a few.

A Closer Look

Why Local Government Matters

Some problems are too big for one person. A street might be too busy. It might not be safe. A new stop sign would help. The town is in charge of roads. So, people can tell their council member. Then the town can put up a stop sign.

Chapter 4

One Job

Some local governments have just one job. A school board is one kind. Board members listen to the community. Then they decide how schools are run.

Different places have different needs. For example, an area might get wildfires. It might have a fire board. The board has only one job. It works on fires. It might hire more firefighters.

Did You Know? Some boards take care of lakes or forests.

Examples of Local Government

FOCUS ON
Local Governments

Write your answers on a separate piece of paper.

1. Write a few sentences describing things local governments do.

2. Would you want to meet the leader of your town or city? Why or why not?

3. What is the leader of a city or town often called?
   - A. a board
   - B. a mayor
   - C. a county

4. What is one difference between a county and a fire board?
   - A. A fire board has only one job.
   - B. A county has only one job.
   - C. A fire board is not a kind of local government.

Answer key on page 24.

Glossary

board
A group that runs a local government.

councils
Groups that make rules for larger groups of people.

election
When people vote for who they want in a government job.

government
The people and groups that run a city, state, tribe, or country.

laws
Rules made by governments.

local
Having to do with one place.

represent
To speak and act on behalf of a person or group.

taxes
Money people pay to their government.

To Learn More

BOOKS

Alexander, Vincent. *Local Government*. Minneapolis: Jump!, 2019.

Ventura, Marne. *Government and Community*. Minneapolis: Abdo Publishing, 2019.

NOTE TO EDUCATORS

Visit **www.focusreaders.com** to find lesson plans, activities, links, and other resources related to this title.

Index

C
counties, 9–10, 13, 21

M
mayors, 13–14

S
school boards, 19, 21

T
towns, 13–14, 16, 21

Answer Key: 1. Answers will vary; **2.** Answers will vary; **3.** B; **4.** A